Positive Affirmations for Black Kids

Quick and Powerful Stories to Uplift
Self-Esteem, Inspire a Positive Mindset,
and Nurtural Cultural Pride and
Emotional Strength

Contents

Introduction

The Power of Words

"Words are like magic spells—they can shape how you see yourself and the world around you! Before we dive into this book, think about this: has anyone ever said something that made you feel like a superhero, full of confidence and strength? And what about the words you say to yourself? Believe it or not, positive affirmations are like secret superpowers—they can make you braver, kinder, and stronger. Ready to discover how the right words can unlock your full potential? Let's get started on this adventure!"

Let me tell you a story. There was a girl named Maya who lived in a big, bustling city. She had dreams that soared higher than the tallest building, but some days, those dreams felt heavy, like carrying a backpack full of bricks. One day, Maya's grandmother handed her a small notebook. "Write your dreams and truths here," she said. "They'll help you feel lighter."

Maya started writing. She wrote things like, "I am strong," and "I am worthy." Each word made her feel braver, like she could face the world, no matter what. Her notebook became her superpower, and those words gave her the strength to stand tall when the world tried to make her feel small.

This book is your notebook. Just like Maya found her strength in her words, you'll find yours here. This book is full of affirmations, stories, and ideas to help you see how amazing you truly are. **Affirmations** are **simple, powerful sentences you can say to yourself every day.** They can help you feel braver, kinder to yourself, and more confident.

Why are affirmations important? Because the way you talk to yourself matters. When you say good things about yourself, it's like planting seeds that grow into strong, beautiful trees. For Black kids, this is especially important. The world doesn't always tell the right stories about who you are or where you come from. But you have the power to tell your own story—a story full of pride, beauty, and strength.

This book is also a celebration of your roots, your culture, and your heritage. You'll learn about some incredible people from history and some incredible young people of today who have overcome challenges and made a difference. You'll see how their stories connect to yours and discover the amazing power you hold inside.

Here's what's inside:

- **Embracing Your Culture**: Know and treasure your family stories.

- **Building Confidence**: Learn how to feel proud of who you are.

- **Finding Resilience**: Discover how to bounce back when life gets tough.

- **Creating Community**: Explore how to find your people and support each other.

- **Dreaming Big**: Learn to reach for the stars without fear.

Each chapter will show you the way, step by step, with stories to inspire you, affirmations to say to yourself out loud, and tips to help you grow. You'll meet real-life Black heroes, some that are your age, who prove that you can make a difference, too.

My hope is that this book becomes a place you turn to when you need a reminder of how powerful and special you are. So, let's get started on this journey together. Open these pages with an open heart, and let's uncover the strength and beauty that lies within you.

Chapter 1
Embrace Your Culture

Have you ever heard your grandma tell the same stories over and over? Maybe she talks about the neighborhood she grew up in or the challenges she faced when she was your age. Those stories aren't just words – they are a part of your history, just like pieces of a puzzle that fit together to show where you come from and who you are.

This is your culture and is what makes your family special. Think of your culture as a treasure chest, filled with traditions, stories, music, and lessons passed down through generations. For example, some families celebrate Kwanzaa, lighting candles and sharing stories about their ancestors. Others might have recipes, like Grandma's famous sweet potato pie, that have been passed from one generation to the next.

In this chapter, we'll jump right into the beauty of your heritage and learn how to celebrate it every day!

Celebrating Your Heritage: Affirmations for Cultural Pride

Black culture is full of amazing traditions, art, and stories that have shaped the world. Did you know that jazz and hip-hop—two of the most popular music styles—were created by Black artists? Jazz started in New Orleans, where musicians like Louis Armstrong and Duke Ellington made music exciting with their cool rhythms and melodies. Hip-hop began in the Bronx, where DJs, rappers, and breakdancers teamed up to create a fresh sound and an awesome cultural movement. Today, both jazz and hip-hop inspire people all around the world!

Did you know Black culture has brought us inventions that changed the world? Garrett Morgan, a brilliant Black inventor, gave us the traffic light, making roads safer for everyone. Sarah Boone made ironing way easier by improving the ironing board. And guess what? George Washington Carver came up with hundreds of cool uses for peanuts—yep, even peanut butter! Oh, and Madam C.J. Walker? She became the first self-made female millionaire—talk about inspiring! Their stories prove that Black excellence is everywhere.

But it doesn't stop there! Black writers, poets, and artists have also changed the game with their incredible creativity. Maya Angelou and Langston Hughes wrote powerful stories that filled people with hope and courage. Jean-Michel Basquiat painted bold, colorful art that celebrated the beauty of Black life and culture. Black culture is packed with amazing stories of strength, creativity, and resilience that inspire us to dream big and shine bright!

Try these affirmations to feel proud of your roots:

- "I am proud of my heritage."

- "My culture is my strength."

- "I am part of a story of resilience and greatness."

Take it to the next level-

Think about a family tradition you have, like cooking a special dish or celebrating a holiday in a unique way. These moments connect you to your roots. Write them down or draw a picture to celebrate them.

The Power of Traditional Hairstyles: Affirmations for Self-Expression

Your hair is your crown, and it's as unique as you are. For centuries, Black hairstyles like braids, cornrows, and afros have been more than just styles—they're symbols of beauty, pride, and history.

But, did you know that braids have been used for more than just looking beautiful? In the past, they had special meanings and were even used to help people! Here is how braids told stories and kept traditions alive:

1. **Secret Maps**: Long ago, braids were sometimes woven into patterns that looked like maps or escape routes. These designs helped enslaved individuals find their way to freedom, leading them to safe places. The patterns in the braids acted like a secret code that only those who knew could understand.

2. **Family Ties**: In many African cultures, braids showed a person's tribe, family, or social status. The patterns and styles were like a name tag, helping others know where someone came from and what group they belonged to.

3. **Hiding Supplies**: During the transatlantic slave trade, people sometimes hid small seeds or grains in their braids. These seeds could be planted later to grow food and survive

in new places.

4. **Togetherness**: Braid styles that were similar often showed unity and connection within communities. When people wore matching styles, it showed they belonged together and supported one another.

Braids are more than just a cool hairstyle—they're like a crown of strength, creativity, and culture! Each twist and turn tells a story of survival, resilience, and pride, linking the past to the present. Isn't it awesome that something so beautiful can hold so much powerful history? It's like wearing a piece of your heritage every day!

Affirmations to celebrate your hair:

- "My hair is beautiful and unique."

- "I love my curls, kinks, and waves."

- "My hair tells a story of pride and culture."

Take it to the next level-

Look in the mirror and say one of these affirmations while smiling at your reflection. Celebrate the way your hair makes you, you!

Language of Our Ancestors: Affirmations Honoring Linguistic Roots

Did you know that languages spoken by your ancestors carry stories, songs, and wisdom from long ago? From Swahili to Yoruba, African languages are full of rich history and meaning. Learning even a few words from these languages can help you feel connected to your roots.

Words in Swahili (a national or official language in Tanzania, Kenya, Uganda, Rwanda and Burundi, Dem. Republic of Congo, Mozambique, Comoros, and Zanzibar)

- **Harambee** (hah-RAHM-bay) – "Pull together" – used to inspire teamwork.

- **Hakuna Matata** (hah-KOO-nah mah-TAH-tah) – "No worries" – reminds us to stay positive.

- **Malaika** (mah-LIE-kah) – "Angel" – a famous love song.

- **Pole pole ndiyo mwendo** (POH-lay POH-lay n-DEE-yoh m-WEHN-doh) – "Slowly is the way to go."

- **Jambo Bwana** (JAHM-boh BWAH-nah) – "Hello, sir."

Song in the Swahili language:

Jambo Bwana- A cheerful Swahili song often sung in Kenya to welcome visitors. Its lyrics celebrate hospitality and the beauty of the Swahili language. **https://www.youtube.com/watch?v=vUrVeRGo 5lM)**

Words in Yoruba:

- **Ile la wa, ile ni a o pada si** (EE-leh lah WAH, EE-leh nee ah oh PAH-dah see) – "We come from home, and home is where we'll return."

- **A kii şe owo kan fi n f'oko d'ori** (Ah kee SHEH oh-WOH kahn fee FOH-koh doh-REE) – "One hand cannot lift a load to the head."

- **Oriki** (oh-REE-kee) – Praise poetry celebrating family and achievements. These special praise poems or songs cele-brate a person's family history and accomplishments. They make people proud of who they are and where they come from. Here is is example- **"Gratitude"** by Laolu Gbenjo (**ht tps://www.youtube.com/watch?v-fkvW-hCGvLk)**

Words in Zulu:

- **Ubuntu** (oo-BOON-too) – "I am because we are."

- **Umuntu ngumuntu ngabantu** (oo-MOON-too n-goo-MOON-too ngah-BAHN-too) – "A person is a person through other people."

- **Shosholoza** (shoh-shoh-LOH-zah) – A song that means "go forward."

Word in Xhosa: spoken in South Africa, Lesotho, and smaller communities in Zimbabwe and Swaziland

- **Ndingumntu nje** (n-DEEN-goom-n-too n-JEH) – "I am only human."

Greetings:

Molo – Hello (to one person)

Unjani? – How are you?

Ndiphilile, enkosi. – I'm fine, thank you.

Ewe – Yes

Hayi – No

Basic Words:

Enkosi – Thank you

Uxolo – Sorry / Excuse me

Ndicela – Please

Hamba – Go

Funda – Learn / Read

Bhala – Write

The saying: "Ndingumntu nje" (n-DEEN-goom-n-too n-JEH) is translated to "I am only human." This reminds us that everyone makes mistakes, and no one is perfect—it's okay to be human!

Affirmations to honor your roots:

- "I celebrate the beauty of my ancestors' languages."

- "Speaking my cultural language connects me to my history."

- "I honor my past through the words I speak."

Take it to the next level-

Learn a greeting or phrase in an African language and teach it to a friend or family member. Celebrate how these words connect you to something bigger.

Learning from Role Models: Stories of Black Excellence

You've probably heard or read stories about Harriet Tubman, who led hundreds of people to freedom through the "Underground Railroad", or Frederick Douglass, who taught himself to read and became a famous writer and leader. Their courage and strength show us what's possible when you believe in yourself and fight for what's right.

Try these affirmations:

- "I am brave like Harriet Tubman."

- "I am determined like Frederick Douglass."

- "I can make a difference in the world."

Take it to the next level-

Think about someone in your life or history who inspires you. Write a few sentences about why they are your role model. What can you learn from them?

True Story- "Khloe's Kind Heart"

Khloe Thompson was known for two things: her big smile and her even bigger heart. She loved helping people, whether it was holding the door for a neighbor or sharing her lunch with a friend. "Helping makes my heart feel warm," she often said.

But one day, something happened that made Khloe realize she wanted to do even more.

The Question That Changed Everything

It all started on a chilly afternoon when Khloe and her grandma were driving home from the grocery store. As they waited at a red light, Khloe noticed a woman sitting on the sidewalk. She had a thin blanket wrapped around her shoulders and held a cardboard sign that said, *"Anything helps."*

"Grandma, why is she sitting outside?" Khloe asked, her eyes wide with concern.

Her grandma sighed softly. "She doesn't have a home to go to, sweetie."

Khloe frowned. "But where does she sleep? What does she eat?"

Her grandma explained, "Some people don't have the things we have, like a warm house or clothes. It's sad, but we can't always fix it."

Khloe crossed her arms, determination shining in her eyes. "Maybe we can't fix *everything,* but we can *do something,* right?"

Her grandma smiled. "You're right, Khloe. Even small acts of kindness can mean a lot."

A Plan Takes Shape

That evening, Khloe couldn't stop thinking about the woman on the sidewalk. "What if she gets cold tonight?" she whispered to herself. Suddenly, an idea popped into her head.

She grabbed a notebook and started making a list:

- Toothbrushes

- Socks

- Soap

- Water bottles

- Granola bars

By the time she was done, she had created a full list of items people might need to stay clean, warm, and fed. She named her project *"Khloe Kares Kits."*

The next morning, Khloe presented her plan to her family over breakfast. "I want to make care packages for people who don't have homes," she announced. "We can fill them with stuff they need!"

Her parents exchanged a proud glance. "That's a wonderful idea, Khloe," her mom said. "Let's do it!"

The Power of Giving

That weekend, Khloe and her family went shopping. They bought toothbrushes, toothpaste, socks, and snacks in bulk. Her grandma even donated some cozy blankets she had sewn by hand.

At home, Khloe turned the living room into a packing station. She carefully arranged items on the floor like a little factory. Her younger cousins came over to help, turning the project into a family event.

Khloe beamed as she zipped up the first completed kit. "That's one down, a hundred more to go!" she said with a determined grin.

Sharing Kindness

On a sunny Saturday afternoon, Khloe and her family drove downtown with boxes full of *Khloe Kares Kits*. They parked near a community shelter where many people were gathered.

At first, Khloe felt a little nervous. Would the people like the kits? Would they think she was just a little kid trying to play hero?

But when she handed the first bag to a woman bundled in a worn-out coat, the woman's face lit up. "Thank you, sweetheart," she said, her voice cracking. "You have no idea how much this means."

Warmth bloomed in Khloe's chest. "You're welcome!" she said, her nervousness melting away.

The rest of the afternoon flew by. Khloe handed out every last *Khloe Kares Kit*, making sure to smile and say something kind to each person. "Stay warm!" "Take care!" "Have a great day!"

A Movement Begins

On the ride home, Khloe couldn't stop smiling. "We *have* to do this again!" she exclaimed.

Her mom nodded. "We will, Khloe. But what if we ask other people to help too? Your school, our neighbors—everyone."

Khloe's eyes widened. "You mean we could make *hundreds* of kits?"

Her dad chuckled. "Why stop there? You could start a whole organization."

Khloe's mind raced with possibilities. "I'll ask my teacher if we can do a school fundraiser! And maybe the church can help, too!"

Kindness in Action

By the following month, *Khloe Kares* had grown from a family project into a community movement. Friends, classmates, and neighbors all pitched in, donating supplies and helping pack care kits.

Local businesses even heard about Khloe's efforts and offered donations. Soon, she was delivering *Khloe Kares Kits* not just downtown but also to shelters and community centers across the city.

Newspaper reporters came to interview her, and her story even made the evening news. But to Khloe, it wasn't about the attention—it was about the smiles she saw when someone opened a care package filled with love.

"I'm just doing what anyone can do," she said. "Kindness isn't hard—you just have to *care*."

Affirmations:

- *"I can make the world better, one kind act at a time."*

- *"My heart is big, and my kindness makes a difference."*

- *"I can create change by helping others."*

Embrace Your Culture

Chapter 2
Build Confidence

B elieving in yourself is one of the most powerful things you can do. Confidence works like a muscle—the more you use it, the stronger it grows. Let's explore how affirmations can help you see how amazing you really are!

You Are Enough: Affirmations for Self-Acceptance

It's so tempting to compare yourself to others, but here's the truth: *You are enough, just as you are.* Your one-of-a-kind talents, creative ideas, and awesome personality make you special. No one else in the world is exactly like you.

Affirmations to remind yourself:

- "I am enough just as I am."

- "I believe in my abilities."

- "I deserve love and respect."

Take it to the next level-

Write down three things you love about yourself. Keep this list somewhere safe and read it whenever you need a confidence boost.

Recognizing Your Strengths

Sometimes we focus too much on what we can't do and forget to celebrate all the things we can do. Take a moment to think about the things that make you amazing. Maybe you're great at solving puzzles, helping your friends, or creating art. Seeing your strengths helps you believe in yourself.

Affirmations to celebrate your strengths:

- "I am proud of what I can do."

- "I have unique talents to share with the world."

- "I grow stronger and smarter every day."

Take it to the next level-

Make a "strengths poster." Write down or draw five things you're good at. Decorate it with your favorite colors and shapes. Hang it somewhere you can see it every day.

Silencing the Inner Critic

Sometimes, a little voice in your head might say things like, "I'm not good enough," or "I'll never get this right." That voice isn't the real you—it's just fear or doubt trying to hold you back. You can silence your inner critic by replacing those negative thoughts with positive affirmations.

Affirmations to quiet the critic:

- "I am kind to myself."

- "I focus on my strengths, not my weaknesses."

- "Mistakes are how I learn and grow."

Take it to the next level-

The next time you hear your inner voice attack you, pause and take a deep breath. Then say something positive about yourself out loud. For example, if you think, "I can't do this," replace it with, "I am capable, and I'll try my best."

Standing Tall and Speaking Up

Confidence isn't just about how you feel—it's about how you *shine!* Standing tall like a superhero, looking people straight in the eye, and speaking up loud and clear are awesome ways to show the world your confidence—even if your stomach's doing a little flip inside. The more you practice, the more powerful you'll feel.

Affirmations for confidence in action:

- "I stand tall because I believe in myself."

- "My voice matters, and I speak with confidence."

- "I am brave, even when I feel nervous."

Take it to the next level-

Practice standing in front of a mirror. Say one of these affirmations while smiling at yourself. Notice how your body feels when you stand tall and confident.

Learning to Trust Yourself

Trusting yourself means believing that you can make good decisions. It's okay to make mistakes—what matters is that you learn from them and keep trying.

Affirmations for self-trust:

- "I trust myself to make good choices."

- "I learn from my mistakes and grow stronger."

- "I believe in my ability to figure things out."

Take it to the next level-

Think of a time when you made a good decision. Write about it or draw a picture to remind yourself that you can trust yourself to do the right thing.

Celebrating Progress

Confidence grows when you can see how far you've come. Maybe you solved a tricky math problem, learned a new skill, or overcame a fear. Celebrate those moments—they show you're making progress!

Affirmations for celebrating growth:

- "I am proud of my progress."

- "Every step I take makes me stronger."

- "I celebrate my achievements, big and small."

Take it to the next level-

Keep a "confidence journal." Each day, write down one thing you did that made you feel proud. It could be something big, like winning a competition, or something small, like trying something new.

Overcoming Challenges

When you run into something tough, it's totally normal to feel unsure or nervous. But guess what? Challenges are like secret missions—they're your chance to grow and level up! Every time you tackle a challenge, you get braver, stronger, and more unstoppable. Remember, you've got this!

Affirmations for facing challenges:

- "I am strong enough to handle challenges."

- "I grow braver with every new experience."

- "I believe in myself, even when things are hard."

Take it to the next level-

Think about a challenge you're facing right now. Write down three things you can do to tackle it. Then say, "I am brave enough to handle this."

Confidence Role Models

Look around you—there are so many people who show confidence in amazing ways. Think about Serena Williams, a powerful tennis player who won more Grand Slam singles titles (23) than any other woman or man during the open era. Think about Amanda Gorman, who made history when she became the youngest inaugural poet during President Biden's swearing-in ceremony in Washington, D.C.

Affirmations inspired by role models:

- "I can be strong like Serena Williams."

- "I can share my voice like Amanda Gorman."

- "I can inspire others by believing in myself."

Take it to the next level-

Choose a role model who inspires you. Write down or draw three things they do that show confidence. Then think about how you can practice those qualities in your own life.

Sharing Confidence with Others

Confidence is contagious! When you believe in yourself, you can inspire others to believe in themselves too. A kind word or an encouraging compliment can help someone else feel strong.

Affirmations for spreading confidence:

- "I use my words to lift others up."

- "I am kind and encouraging to my friends."

- "Together, we can be brave and confident."

Take it to the next level-

Think of a friend or family member who could use some encouragement. Write them a note or tell them something you admire about them. Notice how good it feels to share positivity!

Your Voice Matters: Affirmations for Speaking Up

Your ideas and opinions are important. When you speak up, you can make a difference—whether it's at home, in school, or in your community.

Affirmations to empower your voice:

- "My voice deserves to be heard."

- "What I say matters."

- "I speak with confidence and kindness."

Take it to the next level-

Share an idea or thought during a family discussion or class. Remind yourself that your voice is valuable.

The Power of "I Am": Transformative Affirmations

The words that follow "I am" are some of the most powerful you can say. They shape how you see yourself and the world around you.

Affirmations to try:

- "I am creative and talented."

- "I am a problem-solver."

- "I am unstoppable."

Take it to the next level-

Create your own "I am" affirmation and decorate it on a piece of paper. Hang it somewhere you'll see it every day.

Overcoming Negative Stereotypes

Sometimes, people might say things about Black kids that aren't true or fair. But remember, you are more than any stereotype. You are full of talent, intelligence, and potential.

Affirmations to break stereotypes:

- "I define who I am."

- "I am capable of greatness."

- "I rise above negativity."

Take it to the next level-

Think about a time when you proved someone wrong by showing your strength or talent. Write or draw about it and remind yourself of your power.

True Story- The Winning Word

Zaila Avant-Garde, born Feb. 9, 2007, was the first Black American winner of the Scripps National Spelling Bee in 2021. Read carefully and look for examples of determination, learning, and perseverance.

Zaila Jones loved words. She loved reading them, writing them, and especially spelling them out loud. Long words with tricky letters like *"serendipity"* and *"ebullient"* made her smile. She would bounce around the house, spelling words she'd seen on signs, in books, or on TV commercials.

"Zaila, you've got words flying out of your mouth faster than I can keep up!" her dad teased one afternoon as she raced through spelling her new favorite word: *"phenomenal."*

"I can't help it, Dad! Words are fun!" she said proudly.

A Big Opportunity

One day at school, Zaila's teacher, Ms. Thompson, made an exciting announcement.

"Class, this year, we'll be hosting our first-ever school spelling bee!" she said. "The winner will represent our school in the citywide competition."

Zaila's eyes lit up. "A spelling bee?" she whispered, barely able to contain her excitement.

That afternoon, she rushed home and burst into the kitchen. "Dad! There's going to be a spelling bee at school! I *have* to enter!"

Her dad grinned. "You were *born* for this."

But as soon as Zaila started practicing, she realized spelling in a competition wasn't the same as spelling words for fun at home. There were hundreds of words she didn't know, and some were so hard they didn't even sound like real words.

Practice Makes Progress

Determined to do her best, Zaila created a study plan. Every evening after dinner, she and her dad would sit at the kitchen table with a giant dictionary. He would call out words, and she would spell them, letter by letter.

"*Procrastinate.*"

"P-R-O-C-R-A-S-T-I-N-A-T-E."

"*Chrysanthemum.*"

"C-H-R-Y-S-A-N-T-H-E-M-U-M."

Sometimes she got the words right, and sometimes she didn't. But no matter what, she never gave up.

"Remember, Zaila," her dad would say when she struggled, "practice doesn't make perfect—it makes progress."

The School Spelling Bee

The big day finally arrived. The school auditorium buzzed with excitement. Parents filled the seats, and students whispered nervously as they waited for the competition to begin. Zaila stood backstage, holding her lucky pencil tight in her hand.

Her stomach felt like it was full of fluttering butterflies. What if she forgot how to spell an easy word? What if she got eliminated in the first round?

"Focus on the letters, one at a time," she whispered to herself, breathing deeply. "You've got this."

The competition began. One by one, the students spelled their words. Some got them right, but others walked off the stage when they missed a letter.

Finally, it was Zaila's turn. She stepped up to the microphone, her heart pounding like a drum.

"Your word is... *exuberant.*'" the announcer said.

Zaila smiled. This was one of her favorite words. She took a deep breath and carefully said, "E-X-U-B-E-R-A-N-T. Exuberant."

"Correct!"

The crowd clapped, and Zaila felt her confidence grow. She was ready for more.

The Final Round

After what felt like hours, only two students remained: Zaila and another boy named Marcus. The competition was fierce, with each of them spelling word after word correctly.

"Zaila, your next word is... *effervescent.*'"

Zaila's mind raced. She had seen this word before but couldn't quite remember how it ended. Her hands clenched into fists as she pictured the page in her dictionary.

After a deep breath, she said, "E-F-F-E-R-V-E-S-C-E-N-T. Effervescent."

"Correct!"

The crowd roared with applause, and Marcus gave her a respectful nod.

Then it was Marcus's turn. His word was *"monochromatic."* He paused, took a deep breath, and began spelling—but he missed a letter.

The room fell silent. It was now Zaila's moment. If she got her next word right, she would win the entire spelling bee.

The Winning Word

"Zaila, your final word is... *'perseverance.'"*

Zaila smiled. She thought about all those late nights she spent studying, how her dad always cheered her on, and how she discovered that every mistake she made just made her stronger and smarter.

"P-E-R-S-E-V-E-R-A-N-C-E. Perseverance."

The auditorium erupted with cheers. She had done it! Zaila was the school spelling bee champion!

Her dad hugged her tight when she ran off the stage, tears shining in his eyes. "You did it, Zaila! I'm so proud of you."

"I couldn't have done it without you, Dad," she said. "We practiced, we struggled, and we *persevered.*"

From that day on, Zaila knew that hard work, determination, and a love of learning could take her anywhere—and no word would ever seem impossible again.

Affirmations:

- *"I believe in myself, even when things get hard."*

- *"I can learn new things through practice and patience."*

- *"Mistakes help me grow and get stronger."*

Build Confidence

Chapter 3
Build Resilience

Most of us learn early in life that life isn't always easy. But it's important to have the strength to keep going. Resilience is like a muscle; it grows stronger every time you face a challenge. Let's take a look at how affirmations can help you bounce back

Build Inner Strength

Resilience starts from the inside. It's the belief that no matter what happens, you can handle it. We can think of resilience kind of like building a house—you need a strong foundation to hold everything together. Your foundation is made of courage, hope, and positive thinking.

Affirmations to build inner strength:

- "I can face any challenge."

- "I am stronger than I think."

- "Every day, I grow braver."

Take it to the next level-

Write down three things that make you strong. Maybe you're great at solving, maybe you are very kind, or maybe you are very creative. Read these aloud to remind yourself of your inner strength.

1. _____

2. _____

3. _____

Handle Setbacks

Everyone faces setbacks, but they don't have to stop you. Imagine you're climbing a steep hill. If you trip and fall, you don't go back to the bottom. You pick yourself up and keep going. That's what resilience is all about.

Affirmations for handling setbacks:

- "I learn from my mistakes."

- "Setbacks make me stronger."

- "I will keep moving forward."

Take it to the next level-

Think of a recent setback you experienced. What did you learn from it? Write about how you overcame it and what you'll do differently next time.

Recent setback-

_____

What I learned from it-

_____

Next time this happens, I will

_____

Resilience Role Models

So many Black leaders and trailblazers have shown amazing strength and courage. Imagine being just 6 years old, like Ruby Bridges, and having to walk to school with U.S. Marshals by your side because you were one of the first Black students at an all-white school. Or think about Nelson Mandela, who spent 27 years in prison but never gave up fighting for freedom and equality. Their stories show how powerful resilience can be!

Affirmations inspired by role models:

- "I am brave like Ruby Bridges."

- "I can overcome challenges like Nelson Mandela."

- "I have the power to create change."

Take it to the next level-

Choose a role model who inspires you. Write their name and three qualities they have that you want to practice in your own life. How can you be resilient like them?

My Role Model is

_____

Three qualities he or she has are

_____

_____

_____

Find Support

You don't have to face challenges alone. Family, friends, and teachers can all be part of your support system. Asking for help is a sign of strength, not a sign of weakness.

Affirmations for seeking support:

- "It's okay to ask for help."

- "I am surrounded by people who care about me."

- "Together, we are stronger."

Take it to the next level-

Think of one person you can turn to when you need help or advice. Write down how they've supported you in the past and how you can reach out to them in the future.

Bounce Back with Gratitude

Gratitude means being thankful and showing appreciation for the good things in your life. It's also about being kind and giving back. Gratitude is like a secret power that helps you bounce back when things get tough. When you focus on what's awesome in your life, it's way easier to stay positive and keep moving forward!

Affirmations for gratitude:

- "I am thankful for the support I receive."

- "Every day brings something good."

- "I appreciate the lessons life teaches me."

Take it to the next level-

Start a gratitude journal. Each night, write down three things you're thankful for, no matter how small. Over time, you'll notice how much strength and positivity gratitude can bring.

True Story- Lighting Homes in Sierra Leone

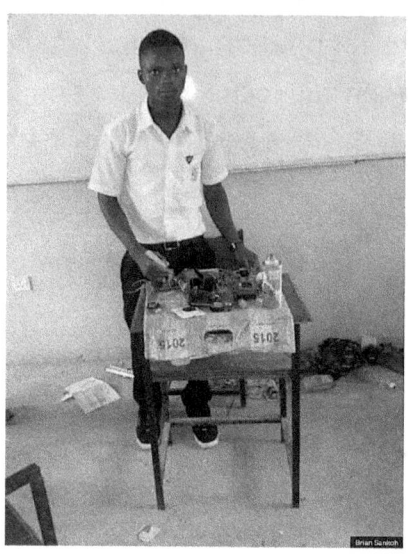

Growing up during the civil war in Sierra Leone, Jeremiah Thoronka had a difficult childhood. Living with his single mother in a slum on the outskirts of Freetown, the country's capital, they relied on dirty charcoal and firewood to generate heat and light.

"I have first-hand experience of growing up without energy or electricity," says Thoronka, who is now 20. "Around 18:00 (6:00 p.m.), the entire neighborhood would be in darkness."

When he was 10 years old, he was awarded a scholarship to attend one of the best schools in the region. "Every day I was moving between two worlds," he says. "There was electricity in abundance at school." But because there was no electricity in his village it was hard for Jeremiah to study at home and the smoke from the firewood often made him and his mother cough.

But Jeremiah was determined to make a difference. He began to think of ways to bring electricity to his village. He noticed that people were always moving—walking, running, and driving. This gave him an idea. What if he could capture the energy from people's movements and turn it into electricity?

With a curious mind and a passion for learning, Jeremiah studied hard and learned about kinetic energy—the energy of motion. He discovered that certain devices could capture this energy and convert it into electricity. Inspired, he decided to create a device that could be placed under busy roads and pathways to harness the vibrations from pedestrians and vehicles.

After many trials and experiments, Jeremiah developed a small device that could generate electricity from the vibrations caused by movement. He called his invention the "Energy Harvester." Excited about his creation, he installed the device on a busy road near his village. To his delight, the Energy Harvester began producing electricity!

With the help of his community, Jeremiah installed more Energy Harvesters around the village. Soon, homes were lit up after dark, children could study in the evenings, and families no longer had to rely on smoky firewood for light. The village became a brighter, healthier, and happier place.

Jeremiah's invention got noticed by other communities and as the news of the Energy Harvester spread, and he was invited to share his idea with those communities facing similar challenges. His dedication and innovative spirit earned him recognition, and he was awarded the Global Student Prize for his efforts in combating energy poverty.

Through hard work and determination, Jeremiah showed that even a young person can make a huge impact on the world. His story inspires others to think creatively, stick with it through challenges, and work to make their communities better places for everyone.

So, the boy who once lived in darkness brought light to his village AND to many others. He proved that with new ideas and heart, anything is possible.

Affirmations:

- *I can solve problems by using my mind and my heart.*

- *Even small actions can create big change.*

- *I have the power to help my community.*

Build Resilience

Chapter 4

Create Community

No one succeeds all on their own. Building a community means finding people who lift you up, support you, and cheer you on. Your community could be your family, your friends, your neighbors, or even people you look up to from afar. Let's talk about how you can create a strong, supportive community around you!

The Importance of Friendship: Affirmations for Kindness and Inclusion

Friendship is one of the most powerful parts of a community. A good friend listens, helps, and stands by you, even when times are tough. And being a good friend means doing the same for others.

Try these affirmations to build stronger friendships:

- "I am a kind and caring friend."

- "I listen and support my friends."

- "I attract positive and uplifting friendships."

Take it to the next level-

Think of a friend who makes you smile. Write down three things you appreciate about them. Then, tell them how much they mean to you—it might make their day!

Lifting Each Other Up: Affirmations for Teamwork

Being part of a team—whether it's for a school project, a sports game, or a community event—means working together to achieve a goal. When everyone helps and supports each other, amazing things can happen.

Affirmations for teamwork:

- "I am a team player."

- "I celebrate the success of others."

- "Together, we can achieve great things."

Take it to the next level-

Think of a time you worked with a group to accomplish something. What role did you play? Write about how you contributed and how it felt to succeed together.

Celebrating Community Leaders: Stories of Impact

Community leaders are people who make their neighborhoods and towns better. Take Stacey Abrams, for example, who worked hard to make sure everyone got a fair chance to vote. Or LeBron James, a superstar basketball player who didn't stop at sports. He opened an elementary school in his hometown of Akron, Ohio, to help kids succeed. These leaders show us that helping others can make a big difference and even change lives!

Affirmations inspired by community leaders:

- "I have the power to make a difference."

- "I can lead by example."

- "My actions can inspire others."

Take it to the next level-

Identify a leader in your community—maybe it's a teacher, a coach, or someone who organizes local events. Write about how they inspire you and what you can learn from them.

Finding Your People: Building a Support System

Your community is made up of people who care about you and want to see you succeed. These might be family members, teachers, friends, or even people you meet through hobbies or activities. Building a support system helps you feel connected and strong.

Affirmations for finding support:

- "I am surrounded by people who care about me."

- "I find strength in my community."

- "I belong to a circle of love and support."

Take it to the next level-

Make a list of the people in your life who support you. Think about how you can show your appreciation for them. Maybe it's writing a thank-you note or simply spending time together.

Giving Back to Your Community

One of the coolest ways to make your community stronger is by giving back! Have you ever tossed a pebble in a pond and watched the ripples spread out. When you help someone, it's like tossing a pebble in a pond—you create ripples of kindness that spread everywhere. Whether you're volunteering, helping a neighbor, or just being kind, every little thing you do can make a HUGE difference!

Affirmations for giving back:

- "I have the power to help others."

- "My kindness makes the world a better place."

- "Giving back brings me joy."

Take it to the next level-

Think of one way you can give back to your community this week. Maybe it's cleaning up a park, donating toys you don't use anymore, or helping a younger sibling with homework. Write about how it feels to make a positive impact. See the appendix in the back of the book for space to write your thoughts.

Community is all about connection, kindness, and care. By building strong friendships, supporting others, and giving back, you can create a community that helps everyone grow and thrive!

True Story- Mari's Mighty Voice

Mari C. was only eight years old when she first noticed something strange about the water in her hometown of Flint, Michigan. She loved playing outside with her friends, but when they came back in, they could never drink from the water fountain at school. Their teachers brought bottled water instead.

At home, it was even worse. The water from the faucet was brown, smelled like metal, and left rust stains in the sink. "Don't drink the tap water," her mom always warned. "It's not safe."

One day, Mari overheard her mom talking to their neighbor about people in Flint getting sick because of the bad water. Mari's stomach twisted. How could something as simple as water make people sick? Wasn't clean water supposed to come from every faucet?

The Big Idea

That night, Mari sat at the kitchen table, watching her mom write a letter to the mayor. Her mom's face was serious, her pen moving quickly across the paper.

"Who are you writing to?" Mari asked.

"The mayor," her mom replied. "I'm asking for help with the water problem."

Mari thought for a moment. "Can I write a letter too?" she asked.

Her mom paused, then smiled. "Of course! Every voice matters, even yours."

Mari grabbed her favorite purple pen and a clean piece of paper from her notebook. She thought hard about what she wanted to say. She wanted someone important to listen, someone who could really help. Then an idea popped into her head—a big idea.

"I'm going to write to the President of the United States!" she declared.

Her mom's eyes widened. "The President? Well, if anyone can help, it's him."

Mari wrote with all her heart:

Dear Mr. President, My name is Mari C., and I live in Flint, Michigan. We have a big problem here—our water is dirty and making people sick. My little brother can't even take baths because his skin breaks out in a rash. We need clean water like everybody else. Please help us!

She signed her name proudly and sealed the envelope with hope.

The Wait

Days passed. Then weeks. Mari checked the mailbox every afternoon, her heart fluttering with nervous excitement. But every day, there were only bills and advertisements—nothing from the President.

One day, after what felt like forever, Mari came home from school to find her mom waving a letter in the air. "Mari! It's here! The President wrote back!"

Mari gasped and snatched the envelope. Her hands trembled as she tore it open.

The letter inside was addressed *to her*. The President thanked her for being brave enough to share her story. He promised that he would visit Flint himself to see what could be done.

Mari could hardly believe her eyes. Her voice had reached one of the most powerful people in the country!

Taking Action

A few weeks later, the whole city was buzzing with excitement—the President was coming to Flint, just like he promised! He met with families, including Mari and her mom. Mari felt a little nervous, but when she shook the President's hand, she stood tall and felt strong. She told him about the struggles her family faced without clean water and how they had to spend extra money just to buy bottled water for cooking, bathing, and drinking.

Her words must have made a big impact because soon after that, help started pouring into Flint. Trucks filled with clean water arrived, donations came from all over the country, and leaders promised to fix the pipes.

But Mari knew her work wasn't done. "We can't stop speaking up," she told her mom.

From that day on, Mari became one of Flint's biggest advocates. She spoke at events, met with important leaders, and helped raise thousands of dollars to bring clean water to the kids in her city. Mari even started her own water drives, collecting donations from people far and wide.

Every time she felt nervous before speaking in front of a big crowd, she remembered her mom's advice from the very first time she picked up her purple pen: *'You have the power to make a difference.'* And that's exactly what she did."

Affirmations:

- *"My voice matters, and I have the power to make a difference."*

- *"Even when I'm young, I can be a leader."*

- *"I will stand up for what's right, even when it's hard."*

Create Community

Chapter 5

Dream Big

Dreams are like stars—they light up your world and show you the way to amazing adventures! No matter how big or small your dream is, it has the power to inspire you and everyone around you. Let's explore how to dream big and take steps to make those dreams come true.

Believing in Your Dreams

Every awesome achievement begins with a dream. Think about inventors, artists, and leaders who changed the world—they all started with an idea and believed in it, even when it seemed impossible. Your dreams can be the start of something incredible too!

Try these affirmations to fuel your dreams:

- "I am brave enough to follow my dreams."

- "My dreams matter, and I will pursue them."

- "I am capable of achieving great things."

Take it to the next level-

Take a moment to close your eyes and imagine your biggest dream. What does it look like? How does it make you feel? Write or draw your dream to bring it to life.

Turning Dreams Into Goals: Making a Plan

Dreams are powerful, but they need a plan to grow into reality. Break your dream into smaller steps. For example, if you dream of being an artist, start by practicing drawing every day or taking a class. Each step brings you closer to your goal.

Affirmations for goal-setting:

- "I am focused and determined."

- "I will take small steps toward my big dreams."

- "Every step I take brings me closer to success."

Take it to the next level-

Write down one of your dreams and three small steps you can take to move closer to it. Start with one step this week and celebrate when you accomplish it.

See an example in the Appendix.

Dream Big, Start Small: Inspiring Stories

Many Black leaders and innovators started with small steps but dreamed BIG!

Mae Jemison, the first Black woman in space, once imagined soaring among the stars—and she made it happen.

Oprah Winfrey started with small steps, growing up in a small town and facing many challenges. She dreamed big, though, imagining a future where she could make a difference. Starting as a local news anchor, she worked her way up to becoming the host of her own talk show, then built a media empire.

Barack Obama is another great example! He started with small steps as a community organizer in Chicago, helping neighborhoods come together to create positive change. But he dreamed big, and through hard work and determination, he became a U.S. Senator and eventually the first Black President of the United States.

Affirmations inspired by dreamers:

- "I can make my dreams come true, just like Mae Jemison."

- "I have the power to inspire others, like LeBron James."

- "I will work hard and reach for the stars."

Take it to the next level-

Write a short story about your dream. Imagine yourself in the future and describe what you've achieved. How does it feel? What impact have you made?

The Power of Visualization

Visualization is like a superpower. When you imagine your dream coming true, it helps your mind believe it's possible. Picture yourself achieving your dream—what do you see, hear, and feel? Use this vision to keep yourself motivated.

Affirmations for visualization:

- "I see myself achieving my goals."

- "I am confident in my vision for the future."

- "I trust the process of reaching my dreams."

Take it to the next level-

Create a vision board. Cut out pictures, words, and symbols from magazines or draw them yourself. Put them on a poster or paper to remind yourself of your goals every day. See the appendix for more.

Facing Fears and Taking Risks

Sometimes, following your dreams can feel scary. What if it doesn't work out? What if people doubt you? Remember, every successful person has faced challenges and doubts. Taking risks is part of the journey.

Affirmations for overcoming fear:

- "I am brave enough to take risks."

- "I learn and grow from challenges."

- "I believe in myself, even when it's hard."

Take it to the next level-

Write down one fear you have about chasing your dream. Then, write an affirmation that helps you feel brave enough to face it. Keep this affirmation where you can see it.

Celebrating Progress

Every step you take toward your dream is worth celebrating. Whether you finish a project, learn something new, or just keep trying, these moments show you're moving forward.

Affirmations for progress:

- "I am proud of how far I've come."

- "Every step brings me closer to my dreams."

- "I celebrate my progress and keep going."

Take it to the next level-

At the end of each week, write down one thing you did that brought you closer to your dream. Share it with someone you trust, and celebrate together.

Dreaming big is about believing in yourself, taking action, and staying inspired. With courage, focus, and affirmations like those above, you can turn your dreams into reality!

True Story- "Moziah's Big Bow-Tie Dream"

Moziah Bridges was nine years old, and had always loved fashion. While other kids played video games or built LEGO castles, Moziah spent hours mixing and matching outfits in front of his bedroom mirror. He liked button-up shirts, shiny shoes, and his absolute favorite—**bow ties.**

"Bow ties make you look sharp," he liked to say, adjusting one around his neck. "When I wear a bow tie, I feel like I can do anything!"

But there was just one problem: Moziah could never find a bow tie that fit his unique style. The ones in stores were boring—plain black, dull stripes, and nothing *cool* enough for someone with his sense of flair.

"I need bow ties that *pop!*" Moziah declared one day. "If I can't find them, I'll make them myself!"

An Idea Takes Shape

Moziah rushed into the living room, where his Grandma Gigi was sewing a quilt. Her sewing machine hummed softly as she guided colorful fabric under the needle.

"Grandma Gigi!" Moziah shouted. "Can you teach me how to sew? I want to make my own bow ties!"

Grandma Gigi smiled. "Well, I've never made a bow tie before, but I reckon we can learn together."

She pulled out her fabric box, filled with scraps of cotton, silk, and patterned cloth from her quilting projects. Moziah's eyes sparkled at the sight of the bold colors and unique designs.

He carefully chose a piece of bright orange fabric with white polka dots. "This one!" he announced.

Grandma Gigi showed him how to measure, cut, and stitch the fabric. It took a few tries—his first bow tie came out lopsided, and his second one was too small—but Moziah didn't give up. He practiced until he created something he was proud of.

When he tried on his first finished bow tie, he grinned from ear to ear. "I *made* this!" he exclaimed, spinning around in the mirror.

The Business Begins

Moziah loved his bow ties so much that he wore them everywhere—school, church, even to the grocery store. People couldn't help but notice.

"Where'd you get that bow tie?" his teacher asked one morning. "It's so stylish!"

"I made it!" Moziah said proudly.

His classmates and teachers were impressed. Soon, people began asking if he could make bow ties for them too. "You should start a business!" suggested his mom.

Moziah thought about it for a moment, then nodded with determination. "I'll call it *Mo's Bows!*"

His mom helped him set up a website, and Grandma Gigi kept the sewing machine running. Moziah worked tirelessly after school, cutting fabric, stitching bow ties, and packing each order with care.

"Every bow tie has to be perfect," he insisted. "No sloppy stitching!"

Challenges Along the Way

Running a business wasn't always easy. Sometimes orders piled up, and Moziah felt overwhelmed. He had to balance school, homework, and his growing company.

One evening, after finishing a huge batch of bow ties, he slumped onto the couch with a tired sigh. "What if it's too much?" he wondered aloud.

His mom sat next to him and squeezed his hand. "Big dreams take hard work, Mo," she reminded him. "But remember, you're not alone. We believe in you."

Moziah nodded, feeling encouraged. "I believe in me too."

A Star on the Rise

As word spread about Mo's Bows, something amazing started happening—newspapers and TV stations began calling! Moziah was even invited to appear on a super popular TV show where he pitched his business idea to famous investors.

Wearing a sharp blazer and his favorite red-and-gold bow tie, Moziah stood tall and confidently shared how he turned his love for bow ties into a growing business. The investors were blown away by his creativity and determination, giving him great advice to help his company grow.

But the coolest moment of all? A famous fashion brand asked Moziah to design a special line of bow ties just for them! He couldn't believe it—his dream was coming true, and he hadn't even hit his teenage years yet!

Giving Back

Even with all his success, Moziah never forgot where he started—or the people who helped him along the way. He created a special collection of bow ties called the "Go Mo! Scholarship Fund" to help kids attend summer camps and leadership programs.

"Business isn't just about making money," Moziah explained during a school presentation. "It's about making a *difference.*"

His message inspired kids everywhere to chase their dreams, just like he did.

Looking Ahead

Today, *Mo's Bows* is a thriving business with customers from all over the world. Moziah still designs every bow tie himself, always thinking about how he can push his creativity further.

"I started with just an idea and some fabric," he likes to say. "If you have a dream, don't wait—start now! You're never too young to make something amazing."

"You don't have to wait until you're older," his mother Tramica Morris said. "If you have a dream and you have a passion, we say go for it."

And every time he ties a brand-new bow tie around his neck, he still feels that same spark of joy, knowing that with a little hard work, creativity, and heart—**anything is possible.**

Affirmations:

- *"I can turn my passion into something amazing."*

- *"Big dreams take hard work, but I'm ready!"*

- *"I can create, build, and inspire others through my talents."*

Dream Big

Conclusion
The Journey Continues

Hats off to you! You've completed this step of your journey of positive affirmations, stories, and activities designed to help you build confidence, resilience, and dreams. But remember, this isn't the end—it's just the beginning. Each affirmation you say, each step you take, and each dream you chase adds to the amazing person you're becoming.

Your culture, your community, and your dreams are your superpowers. When you embrace them, you can shine as brightly as the stars. Keep this book close and return to it whenever you need encouragement or inspiration. The world is waiting for your light—go out there and shine!

Keep the Game Alive

Unlock the Power of Generosity

"*When you lift someone up, you rise too.*" – *African Proverb*

Hey there, amazing reader!

Did you know that sharing your thoughts about this book can help other kids just like you? When you write a review, it's like shining a bright light so other families can find this book and feel inspired too.

This book, *Positive Affirmations for Black Kids*, is all about building confidence, spreading joy, and celebrating the beauty of Black culture. If it made you feel strong, proud, or just plain awesome, your review can make a big difference.

Here's how to leave your review- just scan this QR code-

Reviews are like little love notes to authors—and to other readers too! They remind us why sharing stories like these is so important.

Thank you for being part of this journey to uplift and inspire!

With gratitude,
Keisha Lewis

P.S. Your words matter more than you know. Even a few kind sentences can help spread a message of strength and pride to kids everywhere. Thank you for your kindness!

Appendix

A Few Tools for Your Affirmation Toolbox

C HAPTER 1

Think about a family tradition you have, like cooking a special dish or celebrating a holiday in a unique way. These moments connect you to your roots. Write them down or draw a picture to celebrate them.

CHAPTER 1

Look in the mirror and say one of these affirmations smiling at your reflection. Celebrate the way your hair makes you, you.

- *"My hair is beautiful and unique."*

- *"I love my curls, kinks, and waves."*

- *"My hair tells a story of pride and culture."*

CHAPTER 2

Write down three things you love about yourself. Keep this list somewhere safe and read it whenever you need a confidence boost.

1. _____

2. _____

3. _____

CHAPTER 2

On the next page, make a "strengths poster.' Write down or draw five things you're good at. Decorate it with your favorite colors and shapes. Cut the page from the book and hang it somewhere you can see it every day.

CHAPTER 4

Think of a friend who makes you smile. Write down three things you appreciate about them. Then, tell them how much they mean to you—it might make their day!

1. _____

2. _____

3. _____

CHAPTER 5

Think of one way you can give back to your community this week. Maybe it's cleaning up a park, donating toys you don't use anymore, or helping a younger sibling with homework. Write about how it feels to make a positive impact.

This week I will

_____

After doing this, I felt

_____

Chapter 5

Here are a few samples of Vision Boards.

Use your imagination and creativity to make yours special to you.

Affirmation Toolkit

An **Affirmation Toolkit** is a collection of tools and resources designed to encourage positive thinking, build self-confidence, and inspire personal growth.

Here's what could be included:

Core Components

1. Affirmation Cards

- Small cards with uplifting statements like "I am brave," "I am loved," or "I can handle challenges."

- Could include blank cards for personal customization.

2. Journal or Notebook

- Space to write daily affirmations, reflect on positive moments, or express gratitude.

3. Affirmation Stickers

- Fun, colorful stickers with positive messages for decorating notebooks, mirrors, or planners.

4. Mirror Decals or Dry-Erase Marker

- Inspirational decals or markers to write affirmations on a mirror where they're seen daily.

5. Poster or Mini Inspiration Board

- A visual board with affirmations, inspiring quotes, or images that represent goals and dreams.

Interactive Elements

1. Affirmation Dice or Spinner

- A fun tool where each roll or spin provides a random

positive statement.

2. Daily Affirmation App or QR Code Access

○ Links to affirmation apps or curated playlists with empowering affirmations and meditations.

3. Chakra or Positivity Stones

○ Small stones with engraved affirmations or positive energy themes (e.g., "Courage" or "Peace").

4. Activity Booklet

○ Exercises to teach how to create affirmations, recognize negative self-talk, and replace it with positive thoughts.

Sensory or Motivational Add-Ons

1. Mood-Boosting Items

○ Scented candles, essential oil roller blends, or stress balls to create a calm environment for affirmations.

2. Music Playlist

○ A pre-made playlist of uplifting songs or affirmations set to music.

3. Inspirational Booklet

○ A mini-book of affirmations, inspiring stories, or motivational quotes.

1. Artwork or Prints

- Beautiful illustrations with affirmations to hang up or display.

Customization Tools

1. DIY Affirmation Kit

- Supplies like markers, decorative paper, and washi tape for creating personalized affirmation cards.

2. Digital Template

- Editable affirmation templates for creating custom designs at home.

This toolkit can be tailored for different audiences—kids, teens, or adults—and can be presented in a decorative box, pouch, or bag for easy access. Enjoy putting this together and *feel the love* as you continue to grow in joy, personal confidence, and pride in yourself and your culture!

References

- Britannica. (2024, December 21). *Serena Williams*. https://www.britannica.com/biography/Serena-Williams

- British Broadcasting Corporation. (2021, July 26). *How pedestrians are lighting homes in Sierra Leone*. https://www.bbc.com/future/article/20210713-how-pedestrians-are-lighting-homes-in-sierra-leone

- CNBC. (2021, January 20). *Amanda Gorman's inaugural poem "The Hill We Climb" (full text)*. https://www.cnbc.com/2021/01/20/amanda-gormans-inaugural-poem-the-hill-we-climb-full-text.html?msockid=1453fdeb6be066e83f3be8fc6a8167e2

- HuffPost. (2013, August 6). *Moziah Bridges, 11-year-old entrepreneur, bringing back the bow tie with 'Mo's Bows'*. https://www.bing.com/search?q=huffpost+2013+august+6+moziah+bridges

- National Review. (2021, July 9). *Spelling bee champ Zaila Avant-garde is also a record-holding basketball prodigy*. https://www.nationalreview.com/news/spelling-bee-champ-zaila-avant-garde-is-also-a-record-holding-basketball-pro digy/

- OpenAI. (2025). *ChatGPT* [Large language model]. https://chat.openai.com/

- Wikipedia contributors. (n.d.). *Amariyanna Copeny.* Wikipedia. https://en.wikipedia.org/wiki/Amariyanna_Copeny

- YAYOMG.com. (2020, June 10). *Girl Power, Girls Who Shine Article.* https://www.bing.com/search?pglt=425&q=YAYOMG.com.+(2020%2C+June+10).+Girl+Power%2C+Girls+Who+Shine+Article

- YouTube. (n.d.). *GRATITUDE* . https://www.youtube.com/watch?v=V7_QLurfusc